THE ALL-NEW

SABAN'S

MIGHTY MORPHIN POWER RANGERS™

SCRAPBOOK

by Gale Osborne

SCHOLASTIC INC.

New York Toronto London Auckland Sydney

To our favorite Power Rangers: Harry, Sophie, Michael, and Joshua

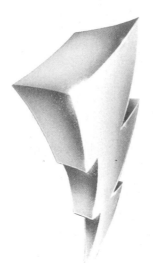

ISBN 0-590-50950-0

Book designed by N. L. Kipnis

12 11 10 9 8 7 6 5 4 3 2 1   5 6 7 8 9/9 0/0

Printed in the U.S.A.   09

First Scholastic printing, April 1995

The Mighty Morphin Power Rangers™ have dedicated their lives to defending the earth against the evil terror of Rita Repulsa™. But nothing could have prepared them for Rita's most diabolical scheme!

The Empress of Evil, Rita Repulsa, devised a devious plan against the Power Rangers. She used her Power Coin to make a teenager from Angel Grove, California, into the evil Green Ranger™.

But evil can never truly defeat good! With determination and strength, and the help and friendship of the Power Rangers, The Green Ranger was able to break Rita's evil spell. He became the sixth Power Ranger!

The Green Ranger was an awesome martial arts fighter. His powerful Dragon Zord™ proved to be a valuable partner for the Power Rangers in gruesome battles with some of Rita's most wicked creations. This came as quite a shock to Rita. Now she had to destroy the Green Ranger!

Rita used the green candle that helped to create the powers of the Green Ranger to lock him in an interdimensional time warp. He faced the most challenging battles of his life.

As if Rita weren't a bad enough enemy, the Rangers soon met up with Lord Zedd™, King of Mayhem. As punishment for Rita's inability to put an end to the Power Rangers, Lord Zedd placed her in a Dumpster and left her to float forever in space! Goldar™ became his favorite henchman.

Lord Zedd created his own Putty People™. They are even more frightening than the old Putties, causing chaos and confusion wherever they appear.

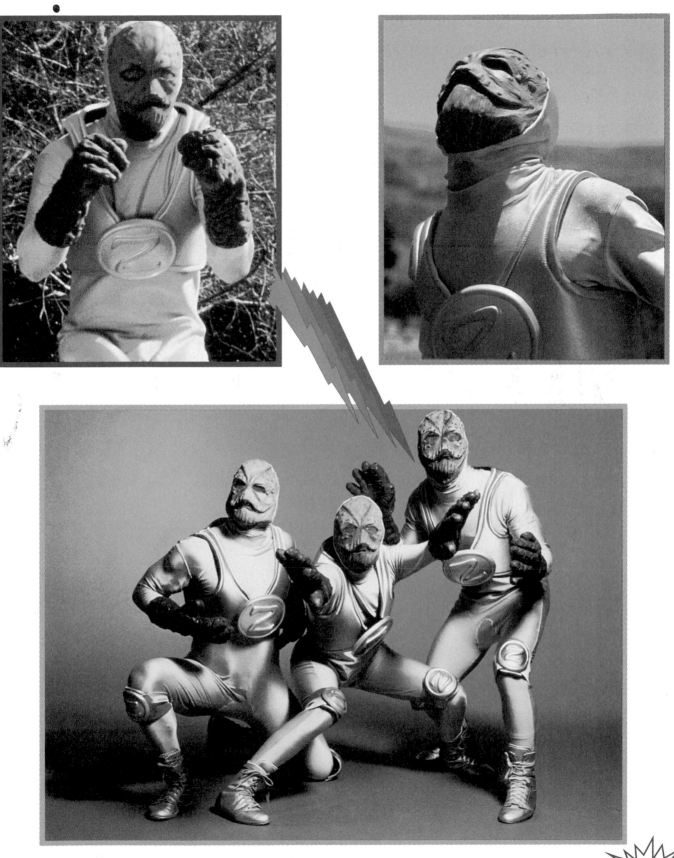

Lord Zedd masterminded a devious plan that drained the Green Ranger of all of his powers. It was curtains for the Green Ranger.

The Power Rangers feared the worst. But once again, Zordan™ and Alpha™ came to their rescue. They created a *new* Power Ranger — one worthy of the responsibility and honor that Power Rangers earn. The White Ranger™ became the new leader of the Mighty Morphin Power Rangers!

The White Ranger
is courageous and
truthful. His powers
are created from the
light of goodness
and can never be
taken away by evil
forces.

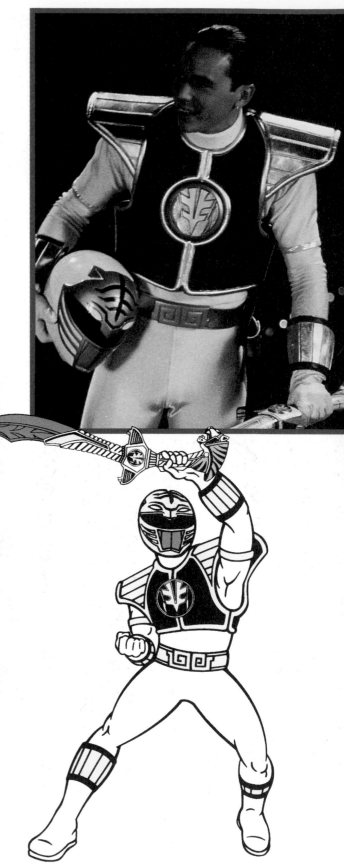

The White Ranger challenges evil with the powerful White Tigerzord™. He carries an enchanted white talking saber sword known as SABA, which assists the White Ranger in battle and controls the new Zord.

No evil warrior is too tough for this new team of superheroes!

RED DRAGON THUNDERZORD™

Lord Zedd proved too powerful for the Power Rangers' old fighting Zords. Zordan was forced to create new, more powerful fighting machines for the teenage freedom fighters.

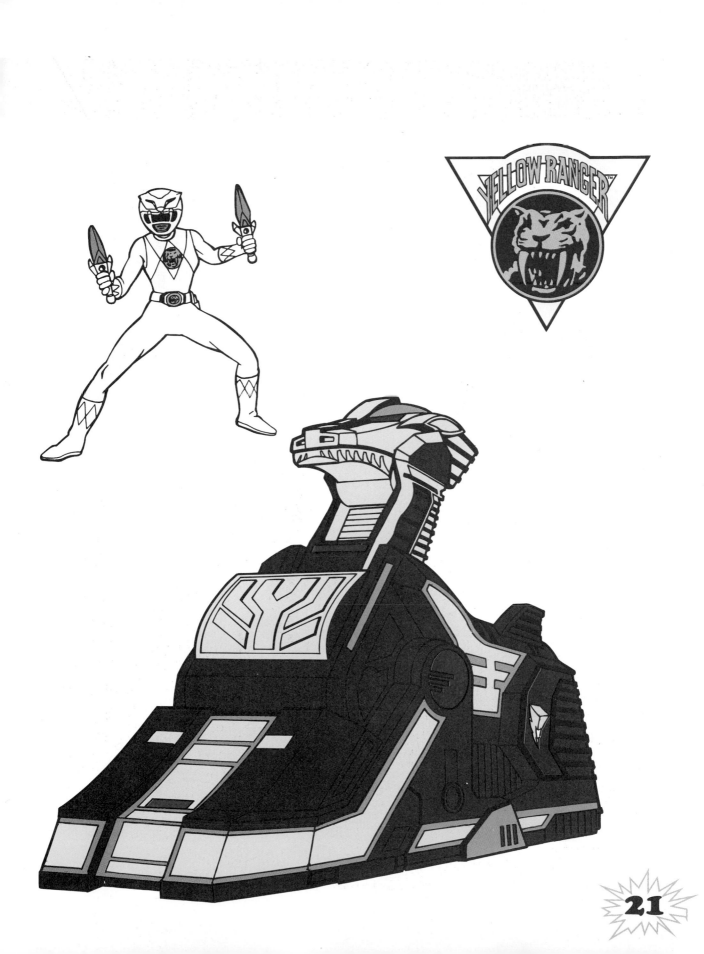

YELLOW RANGER™

21

PINK RANGER™

The Thunderzords harness superior powers on their own. Each one is a mighty fighting machine. Together they become Thunder Megazord™.

These normal teenagers from Angel Grove, California, are ready to morph into action!

It's morphing time!

No evil force, creature, or plot can stop the quest of these young superheroes.

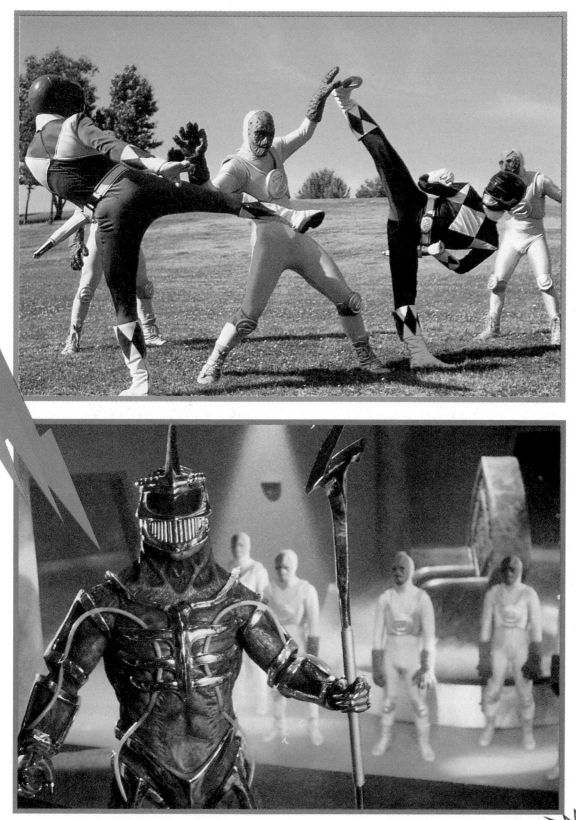

Each of the Power Rangers possesses a unique talent. When combined with the qualities of the other Rangers, they form a force so strong that evil can never defeat them. Here are the Mighty Morphin Power Rangers . . . ready to defend the planet.

Go, go, Power Rangers!